A Special Thank You!

As a special thank you for your book purchase, please log onto the following link below to download your free colouring book to print and enjoy!

Link:

www.amazinglycoolbooks.com/specialthankyou

Copyright © 2020 Natalie Murray

My Fantastic Hair
www.amazinglycoolbooks.com

The moral right of the author has been asserted.

All rights reserved. No part of this publication may be reproduced, stored in a retrieval system, or transmitted, in any form or by any means, electronic, mechanical, photocopying, recording, or otherwise, without prior written permission from the publisher.

Illustration by Sarah-Leigh Wills.
www.happydesigner.co.uk

DMJ Publising
www.dmjpublishing.co.uk

My Fantastic Hair

Written by
Natalie Murray

Illustrations by
Happydesigner

Look what I can do with my hair!
My hair is so flexible. I can create lots of styles.
When I look in the mirror it makes me smile!

I can braid my hair.
I can curl my hair.
I can use my fingers and swirl my hair.

I can straighten my hair.
I can cornrow my hair.
I can use a special comb and afro my hair.
I can leave my hair out!
When I go outside to play it dances about!

As I jump up high
Trying to reach the sky,
My hair shoots up! Like it's trying to fly!

My hair is so very curly and very thick.
I like to wear it just like this.

My hair is short so it is easy to keep neat.
That's why I always look tidy from my head
to my feet!

My hair is light and fluffy.
My curls are quite loose. I look very cool.
When I use my hair gel or mousse

My hair is wavy, shiny and it's also long but my sister's hair is wavy, shiny, short and strong!

We all love our hair because
we can do lots of things:

Ponytails, pigtails and ringlet rings.

We have different hair types, colours and shades. Long hair, short hair, sometimes extended with braids.

Love and look after your hair just like we do.
Your hair is very special just like you.

Other books in the series:

Have you got all 4?

www. amazinglycoolbooks.com

www.ingramcontent.com/pod-product-compliance
Lightning Source LLC
Chambersburg PA
CBHW081400080526
44588CB00016B/2559